Dominie Marine Life

Sponges

Contents

Text by Stanley L. Swartz
Photography by Robert Yin

DOMINIE PRESS
Pearson Learning Group

Where Sponges Live

Sponges make up a large group of **invertebrates** that live in the water. There are more than 5,000 types of sponges. Most sponges live in oceans.

◀ Elephant Ear Sponge

Many sponges are found on **coral reefs**. Some sponges live in shallow, warm water. Other sponges live in deep, cold water.

◀ Barrel Sponge

Their Long History

The oldest skeletal **fossil** ever found was that of a sponge. The first sponges lived millions of years ago. They lived even before the dinosaurs.

◄ Barrel Sponge

What Sponges Look Like

Sponges are very **simple** animals. They have no mouth and no brain. They have no real organs.

◀ **Elephant Ear Sponge**

Sponges attach themselves to shells, stones, or coral reefs. They come in many shapes, sizes, and colors. These colors include green, red, yellow, and purple.

◀ Elephant Ear Sponge

How They Survive

Most sponges are both male and female. There are pores on the outer surface of a sponge. Water and food pass through these pores.

◀ Common Sponge

Sponges filter oxygen out of the water through their pores. They get their food the same way. They have a simple **diet** of bacteria and small organisms.

◀ **Assorted Sponges**

Sponges have few enemies. Some fish, sea slugs, and turtles eat sponges. But most sponges taste bad and can be **poisonous**.

◀ Cally Sponge

Many sea animals live in and among sponges. Sea animals can find protection around sponges. The sponges provide a safe place to hide and live.

◀ **Sea Animals among Sponges**

Commercial Sponges

Some sponges are used for **commercial** purposes. Seventeen types of sponges are used commercially. A sponge has to be at least five inches long to be **harvested** for commercial use.

◄ Common Sponges

A sponge is cleaned before it is used commercially. Only the sponge's soft skeleton is left after the cleaning. Commercial sponges do not look like living sponges.

◀ Cally Sponge

Glossary

commercial: Having to do with buying and selling

coral reefs: Natural underwater ridges made up of coral and minerals

diet: The food that an animal or a person usually eats

fossils: Preserved remains of animals and plants

harvested: Collected, or gathered up, for use or sale

invertebrates: Animals that do not have a backbone

poisonous: Able to cause injury or death

simple: Basic; made up of few parts; not complicated

Index